Congress and
National Security

COUNCIL *on*
FOREIGN
RELATIONS

Council Special Report No. 58
November 2010

Kay King

Congress and National Security

The Council on Foreign Relations (CFR) is an independent, nonpartisan membership organization, think tank, and publisher dedicated to being a resource for its members, government officials, business executives, journalists, educators and students, civic and religious leaders, and other interested citizens in order to help them better understand the world and the foreign policy choices facing the United States and other countries. Founded in 1921, CFR carries out its mission by maintaining a diverse membership, with special programs to promote interest and develop expertise in the next generation of foreign policy leaders; convening meetings at its headquarters in New York and in Washington, DC, and other cities where senior government officials, members of Congress, global leaders, and prominent thinkers come together with Council members to discuss and debate major international issues; supporting a Studies Program that fosters independent research, enabling CFR scholars to produce articles, reports, and books and hold roundtables that analyze foreign policy issues and make concrete policy recommendations; publishing *Foreign Affairs*, the preeminent journal on international affairs and U.S. foreign policy; sponsoring Independent Task Forces that produce reports with both findings and policy prescriptions on the most important foreign policy topics; and providing up-to-date information and analysis about world events and American foreign policy on its website, CFR.org.

The Council on Foreign Relations takes no institutional positions on policy issues and has no affiliation with the U.S. government. All statements of fact and expressions of opinion contained in its publications are the sole responsibility of the author or authors.

Council Special Reports (CSRs) are concise policy briefs, produced to provide a rapid response to a developing crisis or contribute to the public's understanding of current policy dilemmas. CSRs are written by individual authors—who may be CFR fellows or acknowledged experts from outside the institution—in consultation with an advisory committee, and are intended to take sixty days from inception to publication. The committee serves as a sounding board and provides feedback on a draft report. It usually meets twice—once before a draft is written and once again when there is a draft for review; however, advisory committee members, unlike Task Force members, are not asked to sign off on the report or to otherwise endorse it. Once published, CSRs are posted on www.cfr.org.

For further information about CFR or this Special Report, please write to the Council on Foreign Relations, 58 East 68th Street, New York, NY 10065, or call the Communications office at 212.434.9888. Visit our website, CFR.org.

To submit a letter in response to a Council Special Report for publication on our website, CFR.org, you may send an email to CSReditor@cfr.org. Alternatively, letters may be mailed to us at: Publications Department, Council on Foreign Relations, 58 East 68th Street, New York, NY 10065. Letters should include the writer's name, postal address, and daytime phone number. Letters may be edited for length and clarity, and may be published online. Please do not send attachments. All letters become the property of the Council on Foreign Relations and will not be returned. We regret that, owing to the volume of correspondence, we cannot respond to every letter.

This report is printed on paper that is certified by SmartWood to the standards of the Forest Stewardship Council, which promotes environmentally responsible, socially beneficial, and economically viable management of the world's forests.

Mixed Sources
Product group from well-managed forests and other controlled sources
www.fsc.org Cert no. SW-COC-001530
FSC © 1996 Forest Stewardship Council

Contents

Foreword

The U.S. Congress is among the most maligned institutions in the country. In July of this year it registered an 11 percent approval rate—below banks, television news, and health insurance companies—and decrying partisan gridlock has all but displaced baseball as the national pastime. Yet while the perils of this institutional failure are obvious for domestic policy, their consequences for foreign policy are under-explored. The Constitution delegates to Congress considerable responsibility for foreign affairs, including the right to declare war, fund the military, regulate international commerce, and approve treaties. At least as important are such congressional authorities as the ability to convene hearings that provide oversight of foreign policy. A failure to perform these functions could have significant results, leaving the United States hobbled by indecision and unable to lead on critical global issues.

In this Council Special Report, Kay King, CFR's vice president for Washington initiatives, explores the political and institutional changes that have contributed to congressional gridlock and examines their consequences for foreign policy making. Some of these developments, she notes, are national trends that have developed over a number of decades. Successive redistricting efforts, for example, have all but eliminated interparty competition in some House districts, leaving the real competition to the primaries and the most ideologically driven voters. King further notes that the rising cost of elections has increased the time devoted to fundraising at the expense of substantive priorities, and the twenty-four-hour news cycle has decreased the time and incentive for reflective debate. More subtle—but equally important—institutional changes have likewise diminished Congress's effectiveness. A decline in committee chairmen's authority and expertise, tighter control over voting by party leaders, and the relaxation of traditional customs limiting the use of procedural tools to practical ends have all, she writes, led to a breakdown in comity. The consequences she highlights are both broad and significant, from delayed presidential appointments to a poorly coordinated budget process for critical foreign policy areas such as intelligence, diplomacy, and development.

Solving these well-entrenched problems will likely prove impossible, but King issues a number of recommendations that can make a difference. Congress, she writes, should restore traditional restraint in procedural maneuvering, rationalize the budget process, and revamp committee structure in both houses to better address the fast-moving, interrelated threats the United States faces today. The Executive Branch should improve its coordination and consultation with Congress, while, she concludes, the public should hold Congress accountable by becoming better informed on international issues.

As the 112th Congress takes shape during the coming months, *Congress and National Security* will provide sensible guidance to party leaders interested in establishing a more constructive foreign policy–making process. As the complexity and interconnectedness of the world's problems grow, there can be little doubt that such reforms are both timely and desirable.

Richard N. Haass
President
Council on Foreign Relations
November 2010

Acknowledgments

I am extremely grateful to the members of this report's advisory committee, who provided candid and constructive feedback, invaluable insights, and numerous reality checks throughout the drafting process. They include Edith Bartley, Sarah Binder, James Dyer, Richard Fontaine, Daniel Glickman, James Jones, Mark Nichols, Walter Oleszek, Norman Ornstein, and Wendy Sherman. I am particularly indebted to former Congressman Mickey Edwards, who chaired the group with great skill and sensitivity and critiqued the report with the keen eye of a constitutional scholar and Capitol Hill veteran. Three additional committee members—Gordon Adams, Thomas Mann, and Charlie Stevenson—offered indispensable advice on the framing of the study. Daniel Silverberg and Carl Meacham participated in review sessions as observers and provided essential Capitol Hill perspectives. All of the committee members and observers were extremely generous with their time, expertise, and suggestions, but any errors in fact or judgment are mine alone.

In shaping this report, I reached out to many individuals in the legislative and executive branches of government and nongovernmental organizations, and I thank them for their insights and advice. Good friend and CFR member Anne C. Richard was particularly generous with her time and extraordinarily helpful with her advice. In addition, I relied on many excellent studies that address the topic of Congress and national security, including the Project on National Security Studies, the HELP Commission Report on Foreign Assistance Reform, the Princeton Project on National Security, and the U.S. Commission on National Security/21st Century (Hart-Rudman) report, as well as the writings of former Congressman Lee H. Hamilton and many others with expertise on the subject.

This report would not have been possible without the extraordinary research skills of Tim Westmyer, my special assistant at the Council on Foreign Relations, who tracked down every possible lead and provided thoughtful feedback at every stage of the process. The equally talented Kate Collins took over from Tim as my research assistant at the drafting stage and was immensely helpful in editing, rewriting, and fact-checking right up to the publication date.

I am grateful to CFR President Richard N. Haass for his review and comments and for providing the opportunity to write this study. My thanks also go to CFR Senior Vice President and Director of Studies James M. Lindsay, who, as an observer on the advisory committee, provided incisive comments that focused the analysis and arguments in the report. Patricia Dorff receives special mention for her patience and kinder, gentler approach to editing, along with her team of Lia Norton and Elias Primoff. Thank you to Lisa Shields, Anya Schmemann, Melinda Wuellner, Leigh-Ann Krapf Hess, and Lucy Dunderdale in Communications and Marketing for their unparalleled skill in promoting and distributing the report. I am also grateful to Patrick Costello, Elise Letanosky, Thomas Bowman, and Aimee Carter, who assisted in the distribution of this report to targeted constituencies in Washington, DC, including the corporate community. The CFR Library and Research Services department, particularly Marcia Sprules and Laura Puls, were wizards in tracking down sources and suggesting additional reading material. Betsy Bryant and Chelsi Stevens, of CFR's congressional outreach team, offered expert guidance on the subject matter, and interns Alexandra Wilson and Elizabeth Burns provided superb research support.

Kay King

Council Special Report

Introduction

Much has been written, blogged, and broadcast in the past several years about the dysfunction of the U.S. Congress. Filibusters, holds, and poison pill amendments have become hot topics, albeit intermittently, as lawmakers on both sides of the aisle have increasingly exploited these tactics in pursuit of partisan or personal ends. Meanwhile, such pressing national issues as deficit reduction, immigration reform, and climate change have gone unresolved. To be fair, the 111th Congress has addressed many significant issues, but those it has addressed, such as health-care reform and economic stimulus, exposed Americans to a flawed process of backroom deals that favors obstruction over deliberation, partisanship over statesmanship, and narrow interests over national concerns. Although partisan politics, deal making, and parliamentary maneuvering are nothing new to Congress, the extent to which they are being deployed today by lawmakers and the degree to which they obstruct the resolution of national problems are unprecedented. This may explain why Congress registered a confidence level of only 11 percent in July 2010, marking its lowest rating ever in the annual Gallup institutional confidence survey and ranking it last among sixteen major U.S. institutions.[1]

Most of the recent attention devoted to Congress's dysfunction has centered on its impact on domestic issues and has overlooked its effect on national security. Yet Congress's inability to tackle tough problems, both domestic and international, has serious national security consequences, in part because it leads the world to question U.S. global leadership. Reporting from the World Economic Forum in Davos in January 2010, *New York Times* columnist Tom Friedman wrote, "'Political instability' was a phrase normally reserved for countries like Russia or Iran or Honduras. But now, an American businessman here remarked to me, 'people ask me about "political instability" in the U.S.' We've become unpredictable to the world."[2] Furthermore, when Congress fails to perform, national security suffers thanks to ill-considered policies, delayed or inadequate resources, and insufficient personnel. Without congressional guidance, allies and adversaries alike devalue U.S. policies because they lack the support of the American people that is provided through their representatives in Congress.

Given the mounting global challenges the United States confronts, it cannot afford to have a dysfunctional national legislature. To get Congress back on track, it is important to understand both the internal and external sources of the dysfunction and how they affect Congress's national security role with regard to defense, foreign policy, and intelligence. Establishing how a healthy, fully functional Congress should perform in the national security arena will follow from this understanding and lead to institutional proposals to restore Congress as a constructive partner with, check on, and balance to the executive branch on national security matters. The resulting Congress will improve the U.S. image in the world, strengthen its leadership position, and increase its ability to advance U.S. interests and values worldwide. Examining Congress's national security role in a globalized, post-9/11 world presents special challenges. Today, national security encompasses a wide range of issues, including trade, energy, immigration, and border security, that are well outside traditional definitions of foreign policy and defense. These issues, however, are still handled by congressional committees with predominantly domestic responsibilities, such as finance/ways and means, energy, judiciary, and homeland security. Therefore, to maintain an international focus, national security is defined in this context as those issues that fall under the jurisdiction of committees concerned primarily with the U.S. global role: armed services, foreign affairs/foreign relations, and intelligence.

Examining Congress's national security role in a globalized, post-9/11 world presents special challenges. One of them is defining national security in a changing domestic and international environment. Traditionally, national security has been limited to issues of defense, foreign policy, and intelligence and handled by congressional committees focused on the U.S. global role: armed services, foreign affairs/foreign relations, and intelligence. In recent years, however, the definition of national security has broadened to encompass a wide range of issues, including trade, energy, immigration, and border security. But these issues are handled primarily by congressional committees with largely domestic responsibilities (i.e., finance/ways and means, energy, judiciary, and homeland security) that devote little attention to international factors. Therefore, to maintain a focus on the U.S. global role, in the current context, national security will be defined in the narrow sense and focus on issues of defense, diplomacy, development, and intelligence, as well as on the committees that handle them. In the near future, Congress would benefit from an examination of ways to create a committee infrastructure that enables an integrated, strategic approach to national security policy, embracing nontraditional issues and giving higher priority to U.S. economic security.

Another challenge in studying Congress lies in providing objective analysis in the face of the inherent tension between lawmakers' constitutional responsibilities and their political role as elected officials. It is important to recognize that, to some, a legislator's effort to cut funding for health-care programs in Africa is heartless; to others, it is a principled stand meant to reduce government spending. The failure to act on a treaty, though a letdown for advocates, is a positive development for those who oppose the treaty on substantive grounds. Placing a hold on a presidential nominee is obstruction to some, but it can be seen as constructive by others if it results in a desired policy change. Nonetheless, the level of dysfunction and politicization today has led even the most ardent congressional supporters to recognize that the recurring cycle of obstruction and delay, recrimination and revenge, that contributed to the decisions by Senator Evan Bayh (D-IN) and Representative John Shadegg (R-AZ) to retire from office prematurely are beyond "politics as usual" and need to stop for the good of the country.

These two lawmakers leave behind an institution that, despite its problems, includes representatives and senators who are committed, hardworking people with relentless schedules that require them to work long hours, live away from their families, travel weekly, and ask strangers for money. Only a handful of the 435 House members and the 100 senators ever get the opportunity to pass major legislation, achieve a leadership position, or receive the accolades that make the job truly rewarding. Instead, lawmakers are often held in low esteem, derided by the public and the media, and generally scapegoated for problems for which the entire nation shares responsibility. The executive branch, the media, and the public have also contributed to the breakdown in comity and governance in the nation and must do their part to reverse it if the United States is to continue to lead on the world stage. With a new Congress on the horizon, there is no better time to start.

The Congress of Today

The U.S. Congress is a great institution with a rich tradition. It is the branch of government that most directly represents the interests of the American people and most closely reflects the electorate's views. Congress shares significant authority with the executive branch to shape and make foreign and defense policy. The Constitution's framers established the president's explicit authorities in this realm as serving as commander in chief of the armed forces, negotiating treaties, and appointing ambassadors and senior officials. They gave Congress the powers to declare war, appropriate funds, raise and support armies, provide and maintain a navy, and regulate foreign commerce. To the Senate alone the framers bestowed the responsibility of providing advice and consent on treaties and presidential nominees. Since the founding of the republic, this shared authority between the executive and legislative branches has been an "invitation to struggle for the privilege of directing U.S. foreign policy."[3]

Congress, however, has not always lived up to its constitutional role to serve as a partner with, check on, and balance to the executive branch on national security matters. Since the end of the Cold War, its performance has been mixed. In the defense arena, Congress has often functioned smoothly, providing annual authorization bills and consistent funding of the Defense Department and armed services. Yet it has relinquished its authority concerning military base closings to a series of independent commissions, and it is often reluctant to cut wasteful weapons programs, thus undermining its own credibility. On questions of military intervention, it has frequently deferred to the executive branch, failing to provide the scrutiny essential to a successful foreign policy. On matters of diplomacy, development, and intelligence, Congress has been inconsistent and occasionally counterproductive. In its appropriations role, it has failed to provide timely funding for diplomacy and development agencies, delaying the start of programs and the hiring of personnel, thus diminishing U.S. capacity around the world. In its oversight role, despite globalization, it has not overhauled the Foreign Assistance Act since 1985, impeding a coherent approach to overseas programs, and it has resisted making vital structural changes to the intelligence committees, undermining accountability in the intelligence community. In its advice-and-consent role, the Senate has taken ambassadorial and national security nominees as political hostages for long periods of time, depriving the nation of sufficient representation overseas and political leadership in government agencies. It has chosen to allow treaties to languish for years, weakening partnerships and alliances in the process. Equally troubling is the fact that at the very time the complex global arena demands their attention, many lawmakers are increasingly ill-informed about the foreign policy, defense, and intelligence issues on which they vote.

When Congress has focused on the international arena and used its authority constructively and consistently, it has made important contributions to national security. It was proactive in providing support for the former Warsaw Pact nations at the end of the Cold War through the 1989 Support for East European Democracy Act. During the 1991 debate and vote on Operation Desert Storm, Congress played a valuable role in the United States' decision to go to war against Iraq. More recently, despite some serious differences, the Kerry-Lugar-Berman bill—a $7.5 billion aid package for Pakistan enacted in the fall of 2009—was an example of consultation between the political parties and the executive and legislative branches that advanced U.S. interests in an important country at a crucial time. On all these occasions, Congress played its full constitutional role, demonstrating why it is so essential to the advancement of U.S. interests and values around the world.

Although today's institutional dysfunction certainly contributes to Congress's uneven performance on matters of defense, diplomacy, development, and intelligence, it is not the only cause. Congress's role in the national security arena has been eroding over the past twenty to thirty years thanks to globalization and a deeply divided domestic political landscape. The integration of the global economy and the proliferation of imminent security threats posed by the post-9/11 world have produced a more complex and challenging international environment for the United States, forcing Congress to undertake a role for which it is ill-equipped: grappling with a rising number of complex, interconnected issues at great speed. At the same time, the nation's political landscape has been realigning since the 1970s, ushering in deep partisanship, severe polarization, a combative 24/7 media, and diminished civility. Over time, this environment has given lawmakers greater incentive to advance personal and partisan agendas by any means, including the manipulation of congressional rules and procedures. It has politicized the national security arena that, while never immune to partisanship, more often than not used to bring out the "country first" instincts in lawmakers. It has also driven foreign policy and defense matters, short of crises, off the national agenda, marginalizing important issues like trade. Combine this increasingly toxic political climate with an institutional stalemate in the face of mounting global challenges and it is not surprising that Congress has struggled for years to play a consistent and constructive role as a partner to as well as a check and balance on the executive branch on international issues.

POLITICAL LANDSCAPE

The divisive political battles over civil rights and the Vietnam War in the 1960s and 1970s led to a realignment of the two major parties that transformed the American political landscape. The result was a nationwide ideological segregation along geographic lines, with the South and rural areas favoring a Republican Party espousing self-reliance and small government (yet a robust defense budget) and the two coasts and urban areas supporting a Democratic Party promoting economic opportunity for all, government activism, and multilateral cooperation in the global arena.[4] The homogeneity of the parties intensified thanks to gerrymandering, which redrew congressional boundaries to heavily favor the incumbent's party and dilute the opposition's voting strength. As a result, a significant number of House contests today are so one-sided that they are settled in the primaries, which attract the most ardent and ideologically committed voters, forcing candidates to move to the extremes of their respective parties. Once elected, these officials have little incentive to move to the middle, thus diminishing any hope for compromise within the party, let alone across party lines. Consequently, strict party-line votes have been increasing, especially in the House, producing measures that are unable to garner the sixty votes often required to pass in the Senate.[5] The polarization has been spreading to the Senate, which currently includes forty-eight sitting senators who formerly served in the House.[6]

Opportunities for compromise have been further reduced by the permanent campaign. As campaign costs skyrocket, lawmakers must devote more and more time—sometimes as much as 50 percent—to fundraising.[7] At the current pace, victorious candidates must begin looking for support for their next run for office on election night, creating a permanent-campaign environment that results in zero-sum thinking and a winner-take-all attitude. In addition, the two major parties now require lawmakers to raise money for national committee coffers.

Campaign fundraising also has opportunity costs. Time devoted to raising money is time not spent interacting with other lawmakers, denying opportunities to build the collegiality and trust essential for compromise on tough issues. Demanding campaigns also produce increasingly distracted lawmakers, who leave more and more of their legislative and constituent-service duties to staff, diminishing their own ability to understand, much less develop expertise on, the wide range of issues on which they must vote. This also leaves them vulnerable to the thousands of registered lobbyists and special-interest groups who come well equipped to influence lawmakers on behalf of their clients or cause, often polarizing the debate in the process.[8]

Other deterrents to constructive behavior are the 24/7 news cycle and the information technology (IT) revolution. With the advent of cable news, lawmakers quickly learned that public posturing and demagoguery received television coverage at the expense of thoughtful debate and compromise. Similarly, the relentless presence of the electronic media makes deliberation obsolete, forcing lawmakers to respond to blog reports instantly and without careful consideration in an effort to counter negative stories before they "go viral." The Internet has also tended to encourage incivility, enabling rantings and misinformation to spread without the benefit of an editor. Once in the blogosphere, inaccurate information is virtually impossible to correct and is repeated as gospel by both those who do and those who do not know better. Blogs and cable TV news also tend to amplify the echo chamber, reinforcing rather than challenging views already held. This inflamed rhetoric has served to further polarize politics, making it even more difficult for lawmakers to find common ground on issues.

Of course, American voters are not much interested in finding common ground in the current environment. In an unusual turn of the political tide, the "throw the bums out" sentiment in the run-up to the 2010 midterm elections had even incumbents fighting for their political lives. But the voters need to reflect on their contributions when assigning blame for Congress's shortcomings. Uninterested in public policy, especially national security (except when faced with a crisis), typical Americans take little time to understand the issues or study the candidates who are running for office. Often disengaged or easily distracted by straw men or celebrities, Americans get the representation they vote for—if they vote at all. Turnout in the 2008 elections, for example, reached a fifty-four-year high of nearly 62 percent[9]—a weak showing for the world's leading democracy, especially when compared with the 75 percent voter turnout rate in the 2005 Iraqi parliamentary elections, which were conducted at the height of the insurgency there.[10] Voter indifference to international issues usually translates into tepid support for and sometimes even outright hostility toward foreign-assistance programs by lawmakers, as their constituents, understanding little about these initiatives, often oppose them.

INSTITUTIONAL DYNAMICS

The transformation of the domestic political landscape that began in the 1970s brought Congress to the dysfunctional cliff, and lawmakers' intensified manipulation of the institution's rules, practices, and procedures pushed it over the edge. Many of these rules and procedures date back to the founding of the republic and, despite periods of great polarization in Congress, were only occasionally used and rarely abused. But today the motivation to deprive the opposition of victory or to score political points often overtakes the aspiration to serve and problem solve, so rules are used to frustrate and impede action as never before.

Both parties in both houses of Congress are guilty of exploiting the rules at ever-increasing rates. In the Senate, which the framers structured to temper the populist excesses of the House, lawmakers take this right too far by threatening filibusters not just to delay but to completely obstruct action. In the House, which was established to be more immediately responsive to popular opinion but still cognizant of minority views, open debate is often stifled by means of closed and restrictive rules that severely limit or even prevent the bringing of amendments to the floor for debate and a vote. This results in a breakdown of the legislative process, or "regular order."[11] Unfortunately, in a deeply polarized environment, regular order provides the minority with opportunities to play politics and embarrass the majority. As a result, to head off such behavior, the majority feels compelled to advance its legislative agenda by limiting hearings and markups, reducing floor time, and passing legislation with a minimum of debate or delay, thus severely restricting the minority's role.

Over the past two decades in the House, both parties, when in the majority, have deployed a range of tactics, such as closed and restrictive rules, to impede the opposition. Furthermore, at the end of sessions, the House majority leadership often waives the rules to create omnibus appropriations bills, which enable enactment of provisions that the leadership knows could only be approved when wrapped inside a large, must-pass spending bill.

Regular order has been breaking down in the Senate as well. A growing number of filibuster threats have led the leadership in both parties, when in the majority, to limit opportunities for the debate and amendment of legislation that could be filibustered or used as vehicles for poison pill or killer amendments from reaching the floor. Unique to the Senate, which requires the consent of all one hundred members (through a unanimous consent agreement) or sixty votes for cloture to move forward on any matter, the filibuster allows a single senator to block or delay Senate business simply by threatening to engage in extended debate. Rarely used in the Senate's first two hundred years and then usually reserved for major measures, the filibuster came into greater use in the late 1970s. At that time, Senate majority leader Robert Byrd (D-WV) instituted an informal dual-track practice that set aside filibustered bills to allow managers to work out differences as other business was sent to the floor. Senate leaders in both parties have continued the practice, demonstrating the law of unintended consequences. Because the dual-track system has made the filibuster less painful to use, more senators take advantage of it. Majority leaders have responded by filing a cloture motion at the mere anticipation of a filibuster. To avoid floor action that invites filibusters, they sometimes utilize every rule and procedure at their disposal to shut out the minority—and thus impede the very deliberative process that filibusters were intended to promote.

Although cloture motions are filed occasionally for head counting and other purposes, most are intended to overcome a filibuster, and they are therefore a good measure of filibuster threats. According to U.S. Senate data, in the twenty-plus years between 1985 and 2006, when each party controlled the Senate at one point or another, the number of cloture motions filed increased from forty in the 99th Congress to sixty-eight in the 109th Congress. However, after the Democrats took control of the Senate in the 110th Congress (2007–2008), cloture filings soared to 139—a more than 200 percent increase in one year (see Figure 1).[12]

Holds, also unique to the Senate, are informal threats to filibuster that are often registered anonymously (by one senator on behalf of an unnamed other) and almost always honored by the leadership. A practice established when senators had to travel great distances to get to Washington, holds were intended to provide lawmakers with time to review a bill or nomination before it was put to a vote. Recently, holds have been deployed more to prevent presidential nominees or legislation from coming to a vote, as leverage to force action on an unrelated matter. Use of holds as a hostage-taking tactic has been borne out by the fact that, once released, most nominees go on to be confirmed by wide margins. For example, in May 2010, thirty-five nominees had

FIGURE 1. CLOTURE MOTIONS FILED IN THE U.S. SENATE

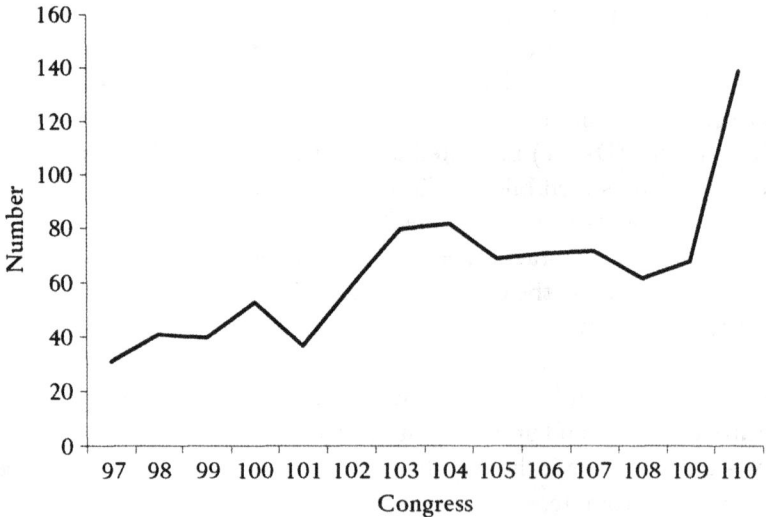

Source: United States Senate, "Senate Action on Cloture Motions," http://www.senate.gov/pagelayout/reference/cloture_motions/clotureCounts.htm.

been on the Senate calendar awaiting a final vote for more than ten weeks. A total of sixteen of these nominees were confirmed by the mid-September recess: fifteen by unanimous consent and one by a roll-call vote of seventy-one to twenty-one.[13]

Although filibusters and holds have received the lion's share of public attention recently, Congress's shortcomings in its critical role of oversight of the executive branch deserve as much attention. Institutional changes in both chambers in the 1970s opened up congressional committees to public scrutiny and gave junior lawmakers some responsibility, striking a blow to the seniority system, thereby reducing loyalty to committee chairmen and engendering greater individualism among members. Their stature diminished, committees, especially those with responsibility for producing the authorization bills that determine policy and spending guidelines for the agencies in their jurisdiction, stopped serving as the principal centers of expertise and authority in their respective realms. Party leaders on both sides of the aisle stepped into the vacuum, increasing their authority (and their staffs) at the expense of committee chairmen, devaluing important sources of congressional expertise and oversight and escalating partisanship in the process.

This is not to say that Congress never engages in oversight of the executive branch. One of Congress's preferred methods of keeping tabs on the executive branch is the reporting requirement. Often a useful tool for gaining insights into policy execution, executive branch agency operations, and compliance with legislative language, reporting requirements have proliferated in recent years. Many, however, are nuisances, ordered by a lawmaker or staff member out of frustration over a lack of consultation or responsiveness from an agency. These requirements usually place onerous tasks on the executive branch, diverting precious time and attention from policy formulation and implementation.

Another method for exerting authority over the executive branch is to attach strings to funding measures to either restrict spending or establish earmarks. The practice of requiring defined amounts of money to be spent on favored projects gives congressional appropriators significant power. Despite widespread criticism of earmarks like the "bridge to nowhere" in Alaska, they represent less than 1 percent of what in fiscal year 2011 is projected to be a $1.4 trillion discretionary budget.[14] Furthermore, earmarks allow lawmakers, who usually are better informed on local issues than executive branch officials, to determine where funds for projects in their own states or districts could be utilized most effectively.

As important as rules, practices, and procedures is the work environment in Congress today. Negative press notwithstanding, the congressional workload can be onerous. Lawmakers travel back and forth to their home bases frequently, often weekly, meeting with constituents, tackling local issues, fundraising, and campaigning. When in Washington, they divide their time among committee assignments, staff briefings, constituent services, and fundraising, as well as legislating. They vote on just about every imaginable issue that affects the lives of American citizens.

Globalization has increased the volume and interdependence of issues facing lawmakers, thus expanding the workload. At the same time, IT has provided constituents with greater, real-time access to their representatives in Congress, exponentially increasing the quantity of constituent mail that congressional offices must tackle. The IT revolution has also made access to information far easier for lawmakers and staff members. Yet the sheer volume of information available in cyberspace puts significant demands on the relatively small personal staffs, who must spend precious time separating the wheat from the chaff. The never-ending news cycle is another omnipresent force that must be managed. The result is significantly increased demands on already limited time and resources. In more collegial eras, lawmakers would often rely on each other for guidance on votes, turning to a colleague with expertise on a particular subject for information. But diminishing civility and rising polarization have led to the breakdown of this informal system, putting more pressure on limited staff to produce the answers or pushing lawmakers to rely on the party leadership for guidance, which contributes to the politicization of the legislative process.

The shortage of collegiality on Capitol Hill is relatively recent. As transportation and communication technologies advanced, travel to home districts became easier, increasing pressure on lawmakers to spend more time in their districts. Over time, rising anti-Washington sentiment and steep housing prices in the national capital area led more and more House and Senate members to leave their families back home. In response, the House and Senate leadership gradually reduced the Washington workweek, scheduling votes on only three days. The result has been a Congress that packs votes, meetings, hearings, and other business into a seventy-two-hour time frame in which there is little time to think, let alone socialize with other lawmakers. This robs members of Congress of both the time to deliberate on issues and the opportunity to develop the relationships that are so critical to forging common ground and compromise.

NATIONAL SECURITY ARENA

Congress's performance in the national security arena over the past twenty to thirty years has been, in a word, uneven. As noted, Congress has had some shining moments, rising to the occasion on major initiatives, such as its recent assistance to Pakistan. But it has been inconsistent in fulfilling its constitutional roles of providing advice and consent on nominations and treaties and overseeing and funding the agencies that have national security responsibilities, especially for diplomacy, development, and intelligence.

OVERSIGHT

One of Congress's most important roles is oversight of the executive branch. When functioning properly, Congress works through its committee system in much the same way a board of directors guides a corporation, providing the executive branch with policy guidance, reviewing its performance, and holding it accountable for carrying out laws as intended. The national security committees use a range of tools for conducting oversight, including hearings, briefings, letters, holds, and reporting requirements. Although the nature of their work requires the intelligence committees to conduct most of their oversight behind closed doors, the armed services and the foreign relations/foreign affairs committees are skilled at holding public hearings on the range of policy issues within their jurisdictions. Each committee, however, has differing success rates with respect to routine oversight of agency programs, operations, and budgets.

One shortcoming that all the national security committees share is their outdated structure. Designed during the Cold War era and updated little since then, the committees that handle foreign policy, defense, and intelligence in both chambers are not organized to adequately address the fast-paced, cross-jurisdictional issues of the world today. Their stove-pipe configurations reinforce divisions and diminish opportunities to work systematically to connect issues of common concern, especially in postconflict environments. The executive branch's current effort to restructure its interagency process to better deal with today's interconnected world, particularly with diplomacy and development, presents Congress with the perfect opportunity to follow suit.

As noted, this lack of strategic coherence is evident throughout Congress, where issues that cut across the domestic and international arenas—such as immigration, energy, and trade—are assigned to committees (judiciary, energy, and ways and means/finance, respectively) that focus primarily on domestic matters. These committees often fail to give sufficient consideration to the international facets of such cross-jurisdictional issues. At the same time, the national security committees, which offer international expertise and perspective, seldom engage directly on these issues, thus reducing their influence and depriving the country of their insights. For example, trade not only opens markets to U.S. exports; it is an important way for developing nations to expand their economies and improve the lives of their citizens, while at the same time reduce opportunities for terrorists to use those countries as breeding grounds or safe havens. Yet this dimension is sometimes absent from congressional trade discussions because the committees of jurisdiction (as well as the congressional leadership) focus primarily on the domestic aspects of the issue.

Comparing the national security committees, it is clear they have differing levels of success. As noted, there has been an imbalance in the effectiveness of congressional oversight of defense activities compared with foreign policy, development, and intelligence matters since the 1980s. Defense oversight in the post–Cold War era has worked, in part because appropriators and authorizers consistently enact an authorization bill on a bipartisan basis that informs the annual defense spending bill. In fact, because they are enacted regularly, defense authorization bills often attract measures, including on foreign policy, that otherwise might not be approved. In addition, the House Armed Services Committee (HASC) and the Senate Armed Services Committee (SASC) appeal to members with seniority and national clout because service on them not only supports the military but enables lawmakers to direct projects that benefit constituents of their home districts or states. The HASC and SASC have also traditionally worked well with their counterparts on the defense and military construction appropriations subcommittees, as well as with the Department of Defense (DOD) and the military, which has improved their effectiveness.

Nonetheless, the HASC and SASC must share in the responsibility for Congress's failure to sufficiently challenge the executive branch on the use of military force. In recent years, acquiescence to President Bill Clinton's troop deployments in Haiti in 1994 and in Bosnia in 1995, along with congressional support for the 2003 invasion of Iraq despite a serious lack of information from the Bush administration about the threat, cost, and likely consequences of the war, represent troubling failures in Congress's exercise of its constitutional authority. This tendency toward deference is often reinforced when the majority in Congress and the president are of the same party. Yet this may be changing; nearly two years into the Obama administration, Democrats in Congress have not been shy about challenging the president's Afghanistan policy.

Critics of the defense authorization process also worry that, in their zeal to support the military, the armed services committees can be less vigilant than they should be, sometimes endorsing unwanted or bloated programs or failing to hold the Pentagon sufficiently accountable for its weapons systems and operations. Here again, changes may be on the horizon; for the first time in decades, disagreements among the legislative and executive branches and the two political parties threaten to derail enactment of the annual defense authorization bill. Disputes about the "don't ask, don't tell" policy and the F-35 alternate engine brought the fiscal year 2011 authorization process to a halt as Congress recessed for the 2010 midterm elections without clear plans to take up the bill in a possible lame-duck session. So it remains to be seen whether the congressional dysfunction has spread to the defense bill.

Oversight by the intelligence committees has been consistently problematic since their inception in the late 1970s. In recent years, these committees have been criticized for lax supervision of the intelligence community (IC), enabling some of the intelligence failures surrounding the 9/11 terrorists attacks as well as the inaccurate assessment of Iraq's WMD capabilities in 2003. Limited expertise, competing demands, fractured accountability, and partisanship all contributed to the intelligence committees' less than rigorous oversight in the first part of the decade. To address the intelligence breakdowns, the committees undertook a reorganization of the IC in 2004, which created the Office of the Director of National Intelligence (DNI), among other things. While well intended, the legislation was hastily reviewed and created a position with little real authority, one that remains awkward to this day.

In the past several years, the intelligence committees have struggled to keep pace with the growing demands for post-9/11 intelligence. Recent

incidents like the Christmas Day 2009 attempted bombing and con-
troversies over alleged electronic-surveillance abuses have left many in
Congress frustrated by a lack of information from the executive branch.
In the aftermath of 9/11, concern about leaks prompted the executive
branch to increase restrictions on congressional access to the most sensitive intelligence information. It limited access to the full membership
of the intelligence committees by significantly expanding the number
of briefings on sensitive covert actions provided only to the "Gang of
Eight"—the chairmen and ranking members of the House and Senate
committees, the House speaker and minority leader, and the Senate
majority and minority leaders. Critics, including many in Congress,
believed the executive branch was overusing restricted notifications to
control information by preventing all members of the two panels from
receiving intelligence essential to performing effective oversight. This
was particularly troubling given that Congress is the intelligence community's only independent source of scrutiny.

A standoff on the access issue developed between the two branches
in 2004, preventing enactment of an authorization measure until September 2010, when the Obama administration and several Gang of
Eight members, including House Speaker Nancy Pelosi (D-CA), ended
the impasse. They cut a deal requiring the executive branch to reveal
new covert-action findings to all members of the intelligence committees within six months, unless the president provides an explanation as
to why limited access is "essential." When limiting access to only the
Gang of Eight, the president must notify the full membership of the two
committees about the relevant finding and provide a general descrip-
tion of the finding, according to the new legislation.

The 9/11 Commission found congressional oversight of the intelligence community dysfunctional in other respects, noting in particular a lack of "unity of effort" caused by a multiplicity of splintered and
overlapping committee jurisdictions in both chambers, which created
redundancies and hampered accountability.[15] While authorizing functions are shared primarily between the intelligence committees and
the armed services committees, many other committees have a piece
of intelligence oversight, including foreign affairs/foreign relations,
homeland security, judiciary, and appropriations. And intelligence
appropriations are made through the defense appropriations subcommittees. Yet Congress chose not to implement the commission's recommendation to establish either a joint House and Senate intelligence

committee or to maintain separate committees in each chamber that combine authorizing and appropriating functions. Both chambers did, however, adopt some of the commission's other recommendations, such as including on the House and Senate intelligence panels members who also serve on the armed services, judiciary, foreign affairs/ foreign relations committees and on the defense appropriations subcommittees. The Senate also ended term limits on committee membership as a means to enhance expertise.

Oversight of the diplomatic and development realms brings with it unique challenges. Thanks to public indifference about international affairs, the typical lawmaker has little incentive to devote time to foreign policy matters and instead focuses on the domestic issues that got him or her elected. Most resist membership on the Senate Foreign Relations Committee (SFRC) or the House Foreign Affairs Committee (HFAC), because neither committee provides opportunities to "bring home the bacon" to constituents and because the foreign policy community is too small and disparate a bloc to wield any meaningful political influence. At the top ranks, the two committees are home to accomplished senior lawmakers from both parties, who issue authoritative reports and conduct serious and productive public hearings on foreign policy matters, but the committees thin out in the middle and lower ranks; in recent years members have begun to rotate off after only brief tenures. One benefit of membership on the SFRC or HFAC is that a lawmaker can use the position to launch a national image for a possible run for higher office or to advance an ideological goal. And some lawmakers find the HFAC particularly attractive because they represent districts with significant ethnic American or diaspora populations that have a special interest in a specific region of the world.

When the broader congressional membership engages in foreign policy or development matters, it usually focuses on narrow, domestically driven issues that overlook the national interest and therefore can be counterproductive. For example, Cuban-American activists in Florida shape policy toward Cuba, which after nearly fifty years has failed to change the political situation there. Armenian Americans regularly persuade lawmakers to support measures that recognize the mass killings of Armenians in the Ottoman Empire in 1915 as genocide. Undertaken despite the protests of Turkey, an important NATO ally in a critical part of the world, the most recent effort was advanced at a time when Armenia and Turkey had been making progress toward reconciliation.

Pursuit of narrow interests can sometimes place other lawmakers and the executive branch in untenable positions, as pro-life lawmakers did for many years. By linking UN dues payments to funding restrictions on assistance to groups that allow abortions as part of reproductive-health programs overseas, they forced pro-choice lawmakers to decide between supporting a woman's right to choose and ending the nation's deadbeat status at the United Nations.

The lack of serious, sustained interest in diplomacy and development issues is shared by the congressional leadership, which often fails, particularly in the Senate, to make floor time in its crowded schedule for authorization bills. The SFRC and HFAC have fallen victim to this dysfunction for years; Congress has failed since 1985 to overhaul the legislation that provides strategic guidance for foreign-assistance programs, instead making piecemeal changes that have often led to incoherence and excessive bureaucracy. Congress has produced a bill to guide State Department activities only sporadically since 2000. This has not been for lack of effort, as the HFAC and SFRC often hold hearings, mark up bills, and vote them out of committee (and, in the House, get them passed by the full chamber), only to see them fall victim to concerns about poison pill amendments or more urgent business on a Senate legislative calendar crowded with ripening cloture motions.

Administrations have been only too happy to live without annual authorization bills for the State Department or foreign-assistance programs because Congress tends to use them to apply provisions that restrict executive action and impose onerous reporting requirements on agencies.[16] Instead, administrations, with the support of Congress, have created discrete programs that provide help to specific regions of the world or tackle particular problems, such as HIV/AIDS. For example, the George W. Bush administration chose to go around the U.S. Agency for International Development (USAID) to create new programs, such as the President's Emergency Plan for AIDS Relief (PEPFAR) and the Millennium Challenge Corporation.

Unfortunately, the proliferation of separate initiatives and the increasing role of domestically focused agencies that have not traditionally had a foreign policy function has led to a splintering of U.S. foreign-assistance programs, which has weakened U.S. development capacity. Currently, international activities are carried out by twelve departments, twenty-five agencies, and nearly sixty government offices.[17] And as worthy as many of these programs are, the lack of a comprehensive approach sometimes has unintended consequences, such as abundant funding to one overseas program (e.g., HIV/AIDS) at the expense of another equally important one (e.g., general public health programs). Should the Obama administration succeed in achieving the goals of its September 2010 Presidential Policy Directive on Global Development and its Quadrennial Defense and Diplomacy Review (due out in December 2010), development will likely be integrated with defense and diplomacy into a comprehensive approach to national security. This promises to provide Congress with a useful template.

PURSE STRINGS

On the funding front, the international affairs budget is included in the nondefense, discretionary spending category, so it competes for dollars with domestically focused budgets. This is an uphill battle made more difficult by the lack of both authorizing legislation and a strong constituency fighting for international affairs programs. As a result, since the end of the Cold War, the international affairs budget has frequently been shortchanged by Congress.

Rarely completed by the end of the fiscal year, appropriations for diplomacy and development are often the subject of a stopgap spending measure known as a continuing resolution, or they are sometimes folded into an end-of-session omnibus bill that is usually passed well after the start of the new fiscal year. This holdup of funds further impedes the work of an already resource-strapped State Department and USAID, which are forced to interrupt or delay programs and the hiring of personnel until funds become available. Such expensive shortcuts as no-bid contracts then become necessary, increasing costs, which are passed on to the taxpayer.[18] Furthermore, in the absence of authorization bills, appropriators frequently insert programmatic language into spending bills often with, but sometimes without, the input of authorizers. This can deny the State Department and USAID the consistent and comprehensive expertise that the HFAC and SFRC offer and undermines the committees' authority by depriving them of a mechanism to elicit cooperation from the agencies they oversee.

Meanwhile, the defense budget has always been somewhat sacrosanct. As noted, for the past several decades, defense appropriators have produced an annual spending bill that is guided each year by a defense authorization bill. Despite occasional differences about a specific weapons program or policy, the funding process has proved highly successful for the Pentagon. But since the FY2011 defense authorization bill is in jeopardy, this may be changing. Furthermore, Secretary of Defense Robert M. Gates, in the face of the nation's spiraling deficits, has begun a budget-cutting effort at the Department of Defense that has some lawmakers concerned about the potential loss of defense dollars for their states or districts.

In the intelligence realm, funding decisions are made by the defense appropriations subcommittees, so IC spending has been guided by individuals with relatively little expertise on intelligence matters, who tend to tie IC funding to trends in defense spending. To address this problem, the House Appropriations Committee recently created an Intelligence Oversight Panel that includes three members of the House Permanent Select Committee on Intelligence (HPSCI) along with ten appropriators. The panel assesses budget requests from the IC and makes recommendations on intelligence funding to relevant appropriations subcommittees, particularly the defense subcommittee. The Senate did not create a similar panel but is undoubtedly tracking the House experience.

Why must the State Department, with its diplomacy role, and USAID, with its development assistance function, beg for attention and funding while the Defense Department receives more than it wants from Congress? Part of the answer lies in the fact that hard power, or military support, is an easier concept to sell than soft power, or diplomacy and development assistance. In addition, DOD represents a large constituency—the military, including active-duty, reserve components, and retirees—with clout. Through the use of earmarks, lawmakers also make sure that defense projects, which provide jobs for constituents, reach just about every congressional district in the United States. Furthermore, the defense industry lobbies Congress very intensely and effectively, expending larges sums of money to win congressional and Pentagon support for its products. In the 2008 election cycle alone, the defense industry spent nearly $24 million on campaign contributions, according to the Center for Responsive Politics.[19]

Although the State Department serves the same constituency— the American people—it has far fewer resources and less muscle than the Pentagon. Foreign Service officers, though well educated and as accomplished and professional as their counterparts in today's military, spend large portions of their careers overseas; they are often viewed by Congress as elitists and are sometimes suspected of advancing a foreign agenda over U.S. interests. As noted, with little constituency in the American electorate, the State Department must battle each year to fund the international affairs account, which represents only 1.4 percent of the U.S. budget, while the Pentagon, with over 18 percent of the U.S. budget (including intelligence funding), fends off demands from Congress to accept funds to continue programs it would prefer to suspend.[20] In addition, soft power is a nuanced and sometimes intangible concept that is hard to explain, especially in a sound bite. Success can be difficult to measure or prove, especially if crises have been prevented. Finally, unlike the defense field, U.S. diplomacy and development programs have few heavy-hitting lobbyists in their corner. Instead, they are supported by effective but less powerful advocacy groups, such as the U.S. Global Leadership Coalition, that often succeed by making the case for the international affairs budget on national security grounds.

Unfortunately, Congress has been slow to recognize that the imbalance between the hard power and soft power components of U.S. national security undermines the nation's ability to formulate and execute missions effectively, especially in increasingly murky postconflict environments like Iraq and Afghanistan. Lacking a joint approach, several jurisdictional clashes have occurred, including the ongoing fight over which department—State or Defense—should have responsibility for assistance programs in a zone of conflict once combat has ceased. Years of inadequate funding have hindered the State Department's and USAID's capacities to deploy large-scale development assistance programs in sometimes nonsecure, postconflict environments, so DOD, which has the resources readily available, assumes these nonmilitary roles, thus raising concerns about the militarization of foreign policy.

This is not a part the military wants to play, not only because development work is not its core competency but also because it recognizes the value of civilian expertise in this arena. Secretary of Defense Gates affirmed this view recently when he said, ". . . you talk to a colonel who's a brigade commander in Afghanistan, and ask him about the contribution a single civilian professional brings a PRT [Provincial Reconstruction Team], and he will tell you they are a gigantic force multiplier. So having civilians who understand this, who know what they're doing, and for whom it is a calling and a profession makes all the difference."[21] Time and again, the evidence supports Gates's point. For example, U.S.

foreign-assistance programs have helped to reduce the burden on the U.S. military by training over 100,000 peacekeepers from around the world in the past five years. They have also assisted in stablizing failing states by improving lives through the support of initiatives such as global health programs that have cut worldwide deaths in children under age five by 50 percent.[22]

In an effort to address this imbalance and win congressional support for adequate funding of diplomacy and development, secretaries of state and defense, including, most recently, Hillary Rodham Clinton and Robert Gates, have gone before Congress in tandem, stressing how hard power and soft power complement each other and require a better balance in resource allocation. But most lawmakers have little time or patience to deal with the long-range and difficult-to-measure outcomes inherent in the diplomacy and development arenas. Understandably, they are more comfortable pursuing the tangible solution of building more weapons systems than making the intangible, time-consuming investment in the people and programs that have the potential to mitigate conflict or rebuild after combat ends.

Of course, the State Department shares some of the responsibility for the lack of congressional support. To be successful on Capitol Hill, career professionals must work with political appointees and civilian personnel to advance the administration's foreign policy agenda. But Foreign Service officers, who are steeped in the culture, history, politics, economics, and language of other nations, often do not seem adequately aware or appreciative of how their own national legislature works, nor do they have the inclination or skill set to engage Congress and make the case for diplomacy and development. Furthermore, working successfully with Congress or mastering the complicated legislative and political processes in the United States is not rewarded in the diplomatic corps. Rising Foreign Service officers have little incentive to understand the unique culture of Congress or develop the relationships on Capitol Hill that are so critical to success there. As a result, few top-ranking Foreign Service officers comprehend Congress and some even disdain it, contributing to what can sometimes be a toxic relationship.

This reluctance to "work" Congress often leads to the withholding of information, which results in communication gaps and misunderstandings in every aspect of the State Department's relationship with Capitol Hill. For example, State Department officials often hold off until the last minute to inform Congress of developments in policy matters or raise concerns about legislative initiatives when it is too late for lawmakers to affect administration proposals before they become public. This undermines the department's ability to gain support from not only its oversight committees but also the broad congressional membership for its policies, programs, funding requests, and nominees.

ADVICE-AND-CONSENT ROLE

The Senate plays a critical, singular role in the national security arena by providing advice and consent on treaties and the president's nominees for senior government positions and ambassadorial posts. The soaring use of holds in recent years, however, has left increasing numbers of nominees in limbo for lengthy periods. One year into the Obama administration, 177 appointees were awaiting confirmation, a significant increase over the 70 nominees pending at the same juncture in the George W. Bush administration.[23] Some of the increase can be attributed to the Obama administration's arduous vetting process, undertaken in anticipation of problems on Capitol Hill, but a large number of nominees were subject to Senate holds. In the Bill Clinton and George W. Bush administrations, the nominees for permanent representative to the United Nations were held up by the Senate for five and six months, respectively, denying the country top-level guidance at an important multilateral institution.

This obstruction diminishes U.S. representation around the world and deprives the country of leadership in vital positions and at critical times, especially at the start of a new administration, when the democratic system is most vulnerable. The delay also confuses and angers foreign partners, who view the lack of timely U.S. representation in their capitals or senior interlocutors in Washington as an insult. Secretary of State Clinton referred to this problem in testimony before the Senate foreign operations appropriations subcommittee in February 2010: "I have to confess that when it came to some assistant secretary positions, some ambassadorial positions, it became harder and harder to explain to countries, particularly countries of significance, why we had nobody in position for them to interact with."[24]

Of course, the Senate has an obligation to fully review presidential nominees, but too many candidates are held up for reasons unrelated to their qualifications. The most flagrant recent example dates to February 2010, when Richard C. Shelby, the senior senator from Alabama, placed a blanket hold on nearly fifty nominees from many agencies. He did this in an attempt to get the attention of the Obama administration regarding two stalled programs that had the potential of bringing significant federal dollars to his state. Once exposed, the glare of media attention persuaded Shelby to release all but three holds. Since the vast majority of nominees subjected to holds eventually get confirmed by large margins, it is difficult for both nominees and the public to take the holds too seriously and fuels the widening cynicism and distrust of Congress.

The abuse of holds has other consequences. The delays and the invasiveness cause some nominees to drop out of the process and discourage other qualified candidates from even accepting nominations so, ultimately, the nation suffers. Congress also undermines its own authority when it abuses holds. Presidents find other ways to move their agendas forward and use their authority to make recess appointments, as was the case with John R. Bolton, President George W. Bush's choice as ambassador to the United Nations. In some instances, presidents choose to skirt the confirmation process entirely by naming special envoys to important national security positions, as President Obama did in naming twenty-four special envoys and special representatives to State Department assignments at the start of his administration.

Just as Congress sometimes obstructs nominations, it occasionally allows treaties to languish. The Convention on the Elimination of All Forms of Discrimination Against Women, submitted in to the Senate in 1980, and the UN Convention on the Law of the Sea, submitted in 1994, provide two examples. First reported out of the SFRC in 1994 and 2004, respectively, they have yet to be considered by the full Senate. Such inaction, although infrequent, nonetheless erodes alliances and partnerships with those nations that have ratified the treaties.

Some lawmakers contend that the failure to take up a treaty represents a deliberate choice to stop a flawed document from advancing. In a rare instance, such inaction may be justified. In most cases, however, the Senate is falling short in its job, especially when one considers that over the past twenty years the executive branch has conveyed only a small number of treaties to the Senate—on average, about thirty-two per Congress, or sixteen each year.[25] On the relatively few occasions that an agreement rises to the level of a treaty, the nation benefits when the Senate takes the time to debate and then vote on the pact, offering its advice, if not its consent. For example, many who supported the

Comprehensive Test Ban Treaty (CTBT) wanted to prevent it from coming to a vote when it became apparent that they did not have the two-thirds majority required for approval. But, as difficult as the outcome was for them, without an up-or-down vote, the issues raised during the debate on the defeated CTBT might never have been aired and eventually addressed to allow for the day when an improved treaty could be resubmitted with an enhanced chance of garnering enough votes required for approval.

Senate inaction on treaties also invites bad behavior on the part of the executive branch: it provides presidents with an excuse to go around Congress and conclude executive agreements that do not require Senate approval on matters that really should have Senate input. As it is, over the past twenty years, on average treaties have accounted for less than 7 percent of all international agreements conducted by the United States.[26]

EXPERTISE GAP

Although 535 individuals serve in the House and the Senate, the shortage of general knowledge, not to mention expertise, on national security matters is serious. Although lawmakers who do not sit on national security committees have never been expected to be experts on defense, foreign policy, or intelligence issues, in earlier eras they took the time to become well enough informed to be able to vote responsibly. Today, this is increasingly difficult to do. Not only is time in short supply, but there is a relatively small pool of experts readily available to advise typical lawmakers or their staffs on an expanding agenda of sometimes arcane global issues.[27]

For unbiased research and analysis, lawmakers often rely on the ninety-one staff members in the Foreign Affairs and National Defense Division of the Congressional Research Service (CRS) as well as staff working on national security issues at the other congressionally mandated support institutions, such as the Government Accountability Office (GAO) and the Congressional Budget Office (CBO). However, budgets at many support agencies have not kept pace with escalating demands for international expertise in the past twenty years, resulting in smaller staffs at CRS and the GAO.[28] And with so much on their plates, staff members in lawmakers' personal offices have limited time to engage experts outside Congress. They can occasionally call on committee staffs, but the talented professionals on committee staffs answer first and foremost to committee members and have limited time to spare for other lawmakers.

Interestingly, the size of national security committees' staffs has not changed significantly in the past twenty years despite the explosion of international issues. According to the CRS (see Figures 2 and 3), the number of professional and support staff serving on the armed services, foreign affairs/foreign relations, and intelligence committees in both chambers was about the same in 2009 as it was in 1989. Both the HFAC and SFRC showed noticeable drops in staff size during that period, but in 2010 they appear to have begun increasing personnel to slightly above 1989 levels.[29] Nonetheless, given the growing complexity and number of issues confronting the country, the size of committee staffs ought to be considerably larger than during the Cold War to enable lawmakers to not only keep up with world events and oversight responsibilities but to directly shape foreign policy.

FIGURE 2. STAFFING OF NATIONAL SECURITY COMMITTEES: SENATE, 1989–2009

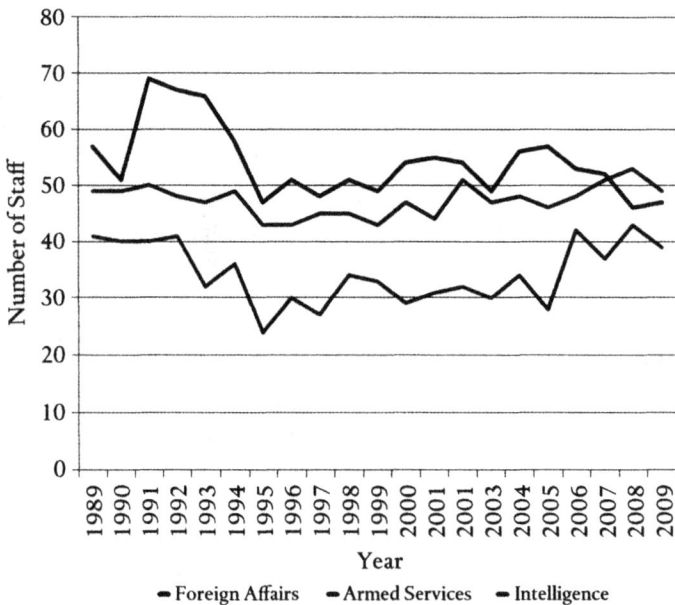

Source: R. Eric Petersen, Parker H. Reynolds, and Amber Hope Wilhelm, "House of Representatives and Senate Staff Levels in Member, Committee, Leadership, and Other Offices, 1977–2010," Congressional Research Service, August 10, 2010, pp. 26–28.

This expertise deficit in Congress is quite dramatic when compared to the size of the workforces at the agencies that the national security committees oversee—600,000 civilians at the Defense Department, 45,000 employees (including foreign nationals) at the State Department, and 8,800 in the USAID workforce. Since much of the work is classified, the actual number of individuals employed by the intelligence community is unknown, but the *Washington Post* reported in July 2010 that an estimated 854,000 people across the nation hold top-secret security clearances.[30] Of course, there is an overlap between this group and individuals with top-secret clearances at DOD, State, and USAID, but the number is nonetheless stunning.

As important, Congress is often impeded by the executive branch in its efforts to become informed about national security matters. Invoking security concerns, administrations resist sharing information on foreign policy, defense, and intelligence matters with Congress and usually reserve consultation for times of crisis. Often, however, the real motivation is to deprive what the executive branch views as an unwieldy group of 535 lawmakers of the opportunity to undermine carefully negotiated agreements or well-developed policies for personal, political, or

FIGURE 3. STAFFING OF NATIONAL SECURITY COMMITTEES: HOUSE, 1989–2009

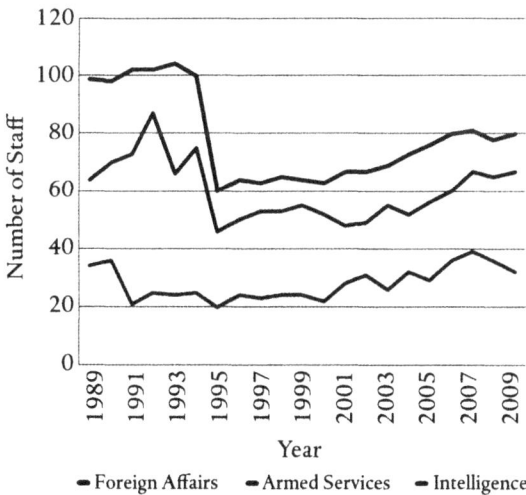

Source: R. Eric Petersen, Parker H. Reynolds, and Amber Hope Wilhelm, "House of Representatives and Senate Staff Levels in Member, Committee, Leadership, and Other Offices, 1977–2010," Congressional Research Service, August 10, 2010, pp. 20–22.

ideological reasons. This sentiment is not without basis. Members of Congress have been known to demagogue issues, sometimes scoring cheap political points at the expense of "foreigners." But lawmakers are elected officials representing the interests of the American people and have a shared constitutional role to play in making national security policy. Unfortunately, the standoff between the two branches regarding information sharing ill serves the nation, because it forces lawmakers to cast ballots knowing too little about the matters they are voting on.

The Congress of Tomorrow

Congress alone cannot change the global environment or the national political landscape, but it can alter the way it does business by reforming the institutional behavior, rules, and procedures that are holding it back from fully discharging its constitutional responsibilities, especially on national security matters. Many of the rules and procedures in both chambers were created in an era of horse travel and the quill pen. They do not reflect the twenty-first-century world. They waste time, drain energy, and are exploited by lawmakers for individual or party advantage at the expense of the national interest.

It is time for Congress to update its rules and return to the practice of using them, along with an orderly legislative process, to advance solutions, not obstruct them. The time is ripe, because there are a large number of relatively new lawmakers in both chambers who want change and are less invested in the current system than their longer-serving colleagues. Currently, forty-nine senators and more than half of House members have been in office for no more than ten years. Thanks to retirements and primary defeats, these numbers will grow by ten in the Senate and by nearly thirty in the House, even before a ballot is cast in the 2010 midterm elections.[31] Combine this development with the deep anger of the American electorate and the daunting challenges confronting the nation and there is reason to believe that reform is not only possible but also essential.

In a perfect world, Congress would serve as an equal branch of government in the national security arena. It would be a fully informed body providing prompt and inclusive action on annual budgets, congressional proposals, and executive branch initiatives; supplying realistic and effective oversight of the executive branch; and offering knowledgeable and timely consideration of treaties and nominations. It would devote time and resources to strengthening its own expertise, and it would commit to engaging in a regular consultative process with the executive branch on matters of national security, especially regarding the use of military force.

If such a Congress were to materialize, it could partner with the executive branch to provide the insights and perspectives on defense, diplomacy, development, and intelligence matters that only the most representative branch of government can offer. It could assist in a transition to a comprehensive, integrated approach to national security that utilizes diminishing resources judiciously and guides policies wisely to diminish external threats; prevent conflicts and reduce the need for military interventions; cultivate new markets for U.S. trade and investment; and improve health, education, and entrepreneurial opportunities in developing states. A revitalized Congress could serve as a proud embodiment of the nation's democratic tradition and values and contribute to maintaining, and, where necessary, restoring U.S. leadership, ensuring the admiration of allies and the respect of adversaries worldwide.

What follows is a menu of options to help Congress start down this path. The period beginning after the 2010 midterm elections and continuing as the 112th Congress gets under way presents the leadership of both parties in the House and Senate with the perfect opportunity to tackle those recommendations—such as reducing each lawmaker's committee assignments—that are achievable in the short term. Both parties can use their postelection party caucus meetings as a jumping-off point to engage first with each other and then across the aisle and up Pennsylvania Avenue to craft new rules, procedures, and practices that can be adopted at the start of the new Congress, no matter which party is in control of each chamber.

PROMPT AND INCLUSIVE BUDGETING AND LAWMAKING

To achieve a healthy and functional Congress that provides prompt and inclusive action on budgets and legislation, both chambers should restore "regular order," ending practices that obstruct and delay as well as shut out the minority. This would require a return to complete adherence to the legislative process: holding hearings, marking up legislation, voting it out of committee, debating and amending it on the floor before a vote of the full body, convening a conference between the two chambers, and voting on the conferenced measure. Too often this orderly process is bypassed in both chambers—in the House for expediency and in the Senate to obstruct. A return to regular order would put both chambers back on track to taking up authorization and appropriations bills in tandem, thus providing, before the start of the fiscal year, the policy guidance and funding that are Congress's constitutional responsibilities. Restoring this process would also curtail the production of continuing resolutions or voluminous, catch-all omnibus bills, which lawmakers are currently forced to vote on with little notice and no opportunity to read, let alone understand, the hundreds of provisions within them.

In the House, a return to regular order would require a reduction in the use of closed and restricted rules and emergency meetings that shut the minority out of the deliberative process. In exchange for opportunities to offer amendments in committee and on the floor and to participate in conferences with the Senate, the minority would have to agree to resist such tactics as regularly offering poison pill amendments intended solely to undermine the process or embarrass the majority. It would be in the interest of both parties to pursue this approach, because it allows the majority to pass bipartisan legislation that has a reasonable chance to survive in the Senate, with its unanimous-consent and super-majority requirements. Regular order also offers the minority a voice and a stake in the process and a claim to being part of the solution rather than part of the problem.

In the Senate, regular order would require changes to the rules to prohibit debate on some procedural motions, limit debate on urgent matters such as appropriations and executive branch nominees, and create a new mechanism to end filibusters on controversial measures:

– *Prohibiting debate.* Current Senate rules allow debate on procedural motions seeking consent to move to the next piece of business, thus opening up additional opportunities to filibuster on a single piece of legislation. The rules should be revised to prohibit debate on these "motions to proceed."

– *Limiting debate.* To allow important matters such as appropriations bills to move forward without denying opponents the opportunity to be heard, a time limit should be set on debate of specific items such as appropriations and executive branch appointments subject to confirmation.

– *Cutting off debate.* There is no shortage of suggestions for reforming the cloture motion. One option would revise the cloture rule to
set declining benchmarks on each subsequent roll call until a simple
majority of fifty-one votes is reached.[32] Another approach suggests
that after a period of time the majority be relieved of the responsibility for ending debate and the onus for continuing debate be shifted to
the minority.[33]

These are just a few of the several filibuster reform proposals that
should be considered because they preserve the Senate's role as the
more deliberative chamber, provide the minority with opportunities to
force debate on important issues, and promise to reduce the number of
filibustered measures in each Congress.

On budgeting issues, Congress would benefit from enforcing the
timetables prescribed in the 1974 Budget Act and requiring that amendments be restricted to spending, as opposed to legislative, matters.
Combined with the proposal to limit debate on appropriations bills, this
could significantly speed up the budgeting process, resulting in fewer
continuing resolutions and omnibus spending bills to fund the government, thus helping agencies to plan and execute their missions effectively. In the national security arena, Congress should adapt its budget
process to handle a unified defense and international affairs budget.

A combination of frustration with gridlock, abysmal approval rat-
ings, a large number of new lawmakers, and the realization that U.S.
global leadership is at stake may be the confluence of events that, for
the first time in thirty-five years, motivates lawmakers to adopt some of
the measures outlined here. These reforms, significant in today's grid-
locked environment, represent a restoration of sound practices for the
most part. Returning to regular order, enforcing the budget process, and
initiating some strategic rules and procedural changes should enable
Congress to better keep pace with the demands of the twenty-first century. These steps promise ultimately to free up floor time for votes on
matters of import that are now crowded out of the schedule, such as
the State Department and foreign-assistance authorization bills, and
should create time to complete all twelve appropriations bills, eliminat-
ing or severely reducing the need for continuing resolutions or omnibus spending bills. Also, they will likely preserve the Senate's role as
brakeman for the House without stopping House initiatives cold. Most
important, they will result in a balanced and integrated national security policy that provides adequate funding to all elements of national

security—defense, diplomacy, development, and intelligence—thus providing not only the military but the civilian capacity to work on programs that promise to advance U.S. goals and values worldwide.

TIMELY AND KNOWLEDGEABLE
ADVICE AND CONSENT

To achieve a healthy and functional Congress, one that offers knowledgeable and timely consideration of nominations and treaties, the Senate must take its advice-and-consent role more seriously by ending its hostage taking of presidential nominees and by voting on treaties within a reasonable amount of time. Swift action on nominees will strengthen U.S. capacity during the critical transition from one administration to another and will alleviate anxieties of foreign countries that feel slighted by the slow arrival of U.S. envoys. Similarly, timely movement on treaties will strengthen the product by allowing advocates and opponents to be heard, and it will reinforce relationships by alerting international partners about U.S. intentions.

Several reforms of the hold process for presidential nominees are worth considering, such as printing the hold request (including the name of the senator making the request) in the *Congressional Record* after one legislative day; requiring a minimum number of senators on a hold request; releasing a held nominee after a sixty-day period; and fast-tracking nominees for a handful of posts identified by the White House as critical to U.S. national security.

In the area of treaties, the Senate would benefit by confronting its responsibilities head-on, taking timely votes on all treaties rather than allowing them to languish. Deferring treaties for decades is irresponsible. The product, and thus the American people, benefit by the open debate that takes place around treaty consideration, so opponents and proponents should make their best case and then subject the advice-and-consent resolution to an up-or-down vote. With the small number of treaties that are on the calendar each year, this would not be too onerous a task. To enhance the process, Congress should undertake the following steps:

– Engage with the executive branch throughout the treaty negotiation and ratification process, insisting that the administration seek the advice and expertise of not just members of the SFRC but also other

interested senators throughout the process and not just immediately
before submission of the treaty to the Senate.

– Vote on the advice-and-consent resolution within two years of the
treaty's submission to the Senate.

REALISTIC AND EFFECTIVE OVERSIGHT

To achieve a healthy and functional Congress that offers realistic and
effective oversight in the national security realm, lawmakers should
update the structure of national security committees, as well as the
authorization and appropriation procedures. Such changes promise to
produce policies that integrate the three pillars of national security—
defense, diplomacy, and development—thus creating a stronger, more
strategic approach to achieving U.S. global objectives. It would also
enhance congressional guidance of U.S. foreign policy and intelligence
matters, resulting in policies that consistently reflect American interests and values. Several steps to consider include the following:

1. *Committee Structure.* The committees in each chamber that have
   primary responsibility for oversight and funding of the nation's
   national security would benefit from working together more closely,
   mirroring the trend of the agencies they oversee. Closer cooperation
   without relinquishing jurisdiction could be achieved through any
   number of the approaches outlined below. While the suggestions
   would increase demands on lawmakers' time for additional hearings,
   this could be balanced, for example, by a reduction in committee
   assignments and a decrease in dilatory tactics.

   – Create a joint national security committee of authorizers to
     include the members of the armed services and the foreign affairs/
     foreign relations committees from both chambers. This joint
     committee would meet on an ad hoc basis to hold hearings on
     overlapping issues, consider legislation that is referred to them,
     and coordinate national security activities that cut across multiple
     agencies, inviting in the chairs and ranking members of other rele-
     vant committees based on the issue (e.g., finance/ways and means
     on trade). Such an approach would promote the sharing of ideas,
     information, and expertise and reinforce executive branch offi-
     cials in their efforts to plan and operate strategically.

- Alternatively, create a separate joint national security authorizing committee in each chamber to meet on an ad hoc basis for the purposes outlined above.

- Or, hold separate joint hearings of the existing national security authorizing committees in each chamber on an ad hoc basis for the purposes outlined above.

- Establish, on an ad hoc basis, separate joint hearings of the defense subcommittee and the state/foreign operations subcommittee of the appropriations committee in each chamber to consider issues that cut across their jurisdictions and to better integrate funding decisions on U.S. military and nonmilitary assets.

- Pursue the 9/11 Commission's recommendation that the House Permanent Select Committee on Intelligence and the Senate Select Committee on Intelligence (SSCI) create a joint committee or keep separate committees but combine authorizing and appropriating powers.

2. *Legislation*

- Diplomacy/Development: A return to regular order in both chambers should ease the way for the timely passage of annual authorization bills to guide State Department operations and foreign-assistance programs. This will require the HFAC and SFRC to wage some tough political battles, but it will increase their stature and help attract and retain senior, experienced members in their middle ranks, which will provide the executive branch with stronger partners in the advancement of U.S. foreign policy.

- Development: Congress should support the work of the HFAC and SFRC in passing the overhaul of the Foreign Assistance Act of 1961, which will help to provide much-needed guidance and coherence to U.S. development policy.

3. *Reporting requirements.* Despite such valuable products as the Quadrennial Defense Review, the increase in reporting requirements on the national security agencies has become onerous and should be reduced to free up valuable agency resources.

- Each authorizing committee should review the reporting requirements for the agency it oversees, sunset outdated or unnecessary reports, and, in consultation with that agency, set a reasonable ceiling for annual reports.

FULLY INFORMED BODY

The proliferation and interconnection of global issues and the demands of a 24/7, wired world require greater, more nuanced expertise. Congress should consider several steps to increase its own expertise in the national security realm, so that it can become a true partner to the executive branch in advancing U.S. objectives around the globe. Some of these steps include the following:

- Reduce the numbers of committee and subcommittee assignments for House and Senate members; this would free up time to allow lawmakers to better focus their attention and to develop greater depth of expertise on specific issues.
- Designate committees as information-resource centers on which all House and Senate members can rely for expertise in their respective areas of jurisdiction. To achieve this goal, Congress should provide funding to hire more nonpartisan and expert staff to serve at these resource centers and encourage the creation of partnerships with universities and think tanks in their respective fields.
- Increase resources for congressional research and investigative support arms, such as the GAO, CRS, and CBO.
- Develop ongoing education programs on national security issues for all members of the House and Senate and encourage meaningful foreign travel to both increase understanding of international issues and build collegiality.
- Assist lawmakers with the development of programs to educate and inform their constituents on national security issues.

Of course, implementation of these recommendations will require Congress to devote more time to its oversight, funding, lawmaking, and advice-and-consent roles, as well as to educating itself on national security issues. Additional time could be found by making just some of the changes to the House and Senate rules, practices, and procedures outlined above. (No doubt campaign finance reform, which is outside the scope of this assessment, would provide lawmakers with more time to legislate as well.) Even so, Congress will also need to increase the time it spends in Washington from three to five days per week, creating a schedule that has the added benefit of helping lawmakers to get to know each other better, thus building the trust needed for compromise.

SHARED RESPONSIBILITY—
THE EXECUTIVE BRANCH

Although the focus of this study is on the national security role of the legislative branch of government, there are several steps the executive branch could take to help Congress in its national security role without violating the separation-of-powers principle. These steps will enhance U.S. national security by addressing differing perspectives and reducing miscommunication, thus helping the two branches to function smoothly and present a united front to allies and adversaries.

- To encourage a strategic, integrated approach to national security matters and to incentivize Congress to follow suit, the administration should offer a consolidated national security budget that ties the 050 (defense) and 150 (international affairs) budgets in a single document and thus captures Defense, State, USAID, and the intelligence community in one integrated account.

- To further advance an integrated approach to national security issues, consider producing a QD³R—a quadrennial review that examines defense, diplomacy, and development operations in relation to each other.

- To improve relationships and increase information sharing, provide incentives to executive branch staff to undertake a rotation in a congressional personal or committee office.

- To improve the particularly strained relationship between the State Department and most lawmakers, require Foreign Service officers on an ambassadorial track to do a rotation on Capitol Hill or in the department's legislative affairs bureau.

- To educate the State Department about Congress, require all entering Foreign Service officers to take a Congress 101 class and study the Pentagon's playbook on how to work successfully with Congress.

The failure to consult is one of the major impediments to successful congressional–executive branch relations in the national security realm because it breeds misunderstanding and distrust. Both branches must commit fully to a consultative process based on mutual respect and a willingness to partner. Time must be set aside for regular meetings and for the exchange of information and ideas at senior levels on a bipartisan basis.[34] The additional time spent on consultations and regular interaction could be more than made up by time saved on miscommunications and misunderstandings and will produce a fully informed national security policy that better reflects the will of the American people. Options include the following:

– Member-level meetings that match senior lawmakers with national security portfolios and senior administration officials, including cabinet officials and senior National Security Council (NSC) staff, to consult on strategic matters before issues become politicized; these should be undertaken in private to ensure the free flow of information and ideas.

– A permanent consultative group that would include members beyond the current national security committees, meet on a regular basis in private, and be given greater access to information, including intelligence data as a means to not only better resolve issues but to build trust and confidence between the two branches on critical national security matters.

– A shadow consultative group that would bring senior congressional and administration national security staff together on a regular basis to share information and ideas, as well as build trust.

– Commitments by the State and Defense departments and the intelligence community to provide information to Congress on a timely and consistent basis to assist lawmakers in making fully informed judgments on national security matters.

SHARED RESPONSIBILITY— THE AMERICAN PEOPLE

The American people must demand more of themselves and more of their representatives in Congress when it comes to national security issues. Americans cannot afford to shut out the world. Like it or not, the United States is more reliant than ever on other nations to help ensure its own prosperity and safety, so global events, especially in the economic and security realms, will have an increasing impact on American lives. Each citizen is responsible for being informed about international issues and understanding the options confronting the nation and for demanding that his or her elected representatives in Congress do the same.

As leaders, lawmakers must get their own house in order first and set the example for the rest of the nation by putting country before personal, local, or party interests. All fixes to the House and Senate rules and procedures will be meaningless without a restoration of the comity, trust, and compromise that is essential to a successful democracy. The challenges to the nation are daunting and must be met with a unity of purpose that commands the full commitment of Capitol Hill and the American people. An informed electorate and engaged Congress are essential to producing the sound policies necessary to successfully address the nation's challenges and exploit its opportunities.

As a lawmaker for thirty-four years and a former chairman of the House Foreign Affairs Committee, Representative Lee H. Hamilton (D-IN) summed up the task for Congress when he wrote in 2002, "At its best, the making of foreign policy can be a creative process that transcends self-interest or the goals of special interests and seeks to advance the nation's broader interests. The job of the congressional foreign policy maker is to forge a consensus that advances the national interest out of the American people's many interests and concerns."[35]

If Congress is able to address the institutional problems that are holding it back and forge a consensus as Lee Hamilton suggests, the country can look forward to a congressional-executive partnership on national security policy that is fully considered and well informed; that is unified, balanced and strategic; and that advances U.S. interests and values around the world. The nation deserves nothing less.

Endnotes

1. Lydia Saad, "Congress Ranks Last in Confidence in Institutions," Gallup.com, July 22, 2010.
2. "Never Heard That Before," Thomas Friedman, *New York Times*, January 31, 2010, http://www.nytimes.com/2010/01/31/opinion/31friedman.html.
3. Edwin S. Corwin, *The President: Office and Powers, 1787–1957* (New York: New York University Press, 1957), p. 171.
4. Thomas E. Mann and Norman J. Ornstein, *The Broken Branch: How Congress Is Failing America and How to Get It Back on Track*, (New York: Oxford University Press, 2008), pp. 11–13.
5. In 2008, House Democrats voted with their party a record 92 percent of the time, while Republicans' party unity average was 87 percent. Richard Rubin, "Party Unity: An Ever Thicker Dividing Line," *CQ Weekly*, January 11, 2010.
6. Data from Sean M. Theriault and David W. Rhode, "The Gingrich Senators and Their Effect on the U.S. Senate," paper prepared for delivery at the American Political Science Association Annual Meeting, July 26, 2010, p. 27, http://www.themonkeycage.org/gingrich%20senators_apsa.pdf; "Terms of Service: Class III—Senators Whose Terms of Service Expire in 2011," U.S. Senate, http://senate.gov/pagelayout/reference/two_column_table/Class_III.htm; "Terms of Service: Class II—Senators Whose Terms of Service Expire in 2015," U.S. Senate, http://senate.gov/pagelayout/reference/two_column_table/Class_II.htm; "Terms of Service: Class I—Senators Whose Term of Service Expire in 2013," U.S. Senate, http://senate.gov/pagelayout/reference/two_column_table/Class_I.htm.
7. In the 2008 cycle, successful House candidates had to raise an average of $1.4 million, or over $700,000 a year, to win their two-year term, more than double the amount needed to succeed in 1994. Victorious Senate candidates in 2008 needed more than $8.5 million to win in their races, requiring them to pull in more than $1.4 million in each year of their six-year term. See "Politicians and Elections: Election Stats 2008," OpenSecrets.org, Center for Responsive Politics, http://www.opensecrets.org/bigpicture/elec_stats.php?cycle=2008.
8. The lobbying industry has grown significantly in just the past decade, with a total of 13,694 lobbyists registered in Washington, DC, in 2009 spending just under $3.5 billion to influence Congress and the federal government. This is more than double the $1.5 billion spent on lobbying activities ten years earlier, according to the Center for Responsive Politics. "Lobbying Database," Center for Responsive Politics, http://www.opensecrets.org/lobby/index.php.
9. "United States Elections Project," Dr. Michael McDonald, George Mason University, 2010, http://www.elections.gmu.edu/turnout_2008G.
10. "Iraq Election Turnout 62%, Officials Say," BBC News, March 9, 2010, http://news.bbc.co.uk/2/hi/8556065.stm.

11. "Regular order" is the lengthy process of subcommittee and committee hearings, followed by bill markups, then debate and amendment on the floor, followed by a final vote. The process concludes with a bicameral conference and votes in each chamber on the final conferenced bill. Although somewhat arduous, the process ensures that conflicting views are thoroughly aired and debated before a vote.

12. "Senate Action on Cloture Motions," United States Senate, http://www.senate.gov/pagelayout/reference/cloture_motions/clotureCounts.htm.

13. For information on nominees pending on the Senate Executive Calendar in May 2010, see Dan Pfeiffer, "Obstruction as a Political Strategy," White House Blog, May 6, 2010. http://www.whitehouse.gov/blog/2010/05/06/obstruction-a-political-strategy. For a record of Senate votes on nominees, see "Presidential Nominations, Library of Congress, Thomas website. http://thomas.loc.gov/cgi-bin/thomas.

14. Walter Alarkon, "Self-Imposed Republican Moratorium Leads to Drop in 2011 Earmark Spending," On the Money: Appropriations (blog), *The Hill*, August 1, 2010, http://www.thehill.com/blogs/on-the/money/appropriations.

15. National Commission on Terrorist Attacks upon the United States, Philip Zelikow, executive director; Bonnie D. Jenkins, counsel; Ernest R. May, senior adviser, *The 9/11 Commission Report* (New York: W.W. Norton & Company, 2004).

16. The State Department is often tasked with a large number of reporting requirements. In FY2009, the department submitted approximately three hundred reports to Congress. Legislative Reference Unit, Bureau of Legislative Affairs, U.S. Department of State, September 23, 2010. Likewise, congressional demands for Pentagon reports have become so numerous (nearly seven hundred in 2009 alone) that Secretary of Defense Robert M. Gates announced in August 2010 that DOD would undertake a comprehensive review of the oversight reports and then engage with Congress on reducing the volume of reports. "DOD News Briefing with Secretary Gates from the Pentagon," U.S. Department of Defense, Office of the Assistant Secretary of Defense for Public Affairs, August 9, 2010.

17. Rebecca Williams, "Understanding the Diaspora of U.S. Foreign Assistance," The Will and the Wallet (blog), Stimson Center, Washington, DC, April 7, 2010.

18. Ian Millhiser, "The Tyranny of the Timepiece: Senate Rules Obstruct Voting to a Degree That Wounds Our Governments, Center for American Progress, Washingon, DC, September 28, 2010, p. 7.

19. "Defense: Long-Term Contributions," Center for Responsive Politics, http://www.opensecrets.org/industries/totals.php?ind.

20. For FY2011 budget data, see the White House Office of Management and Budget, "The Budget for the Fiscal Year 2011 Summary Tables: Table S–1. Budget Totals," p. 2, http://www.whitehouse.gov/sites/default/files/omb/budget/fy2011/assets/tables.pdf. For international affairs budget information, see Jordan Smith, "The International Affairs Budget: Critical Investments in National Security," U.S. Global Leadership Council, January 28, 2010, http://www.usglc.org/2010/01/28; for defense budget data, see "The Federal Budget, Fiscal Year 2011: Department of Defense," the White House Office of Management and Budget, http://www.whitehouse.gov/omb/factsheet_department_defense.

21. U.S. Global Leadership Coalition Annual Conference 2010, Washington, DC, September 28, 2010.

22. "Smart Power Fact Sheet: Keeping America Safe" and "Smart Power Fact Sheet: Demonstrating Our Humanitarian Values," U.S. Global Leadership Coalition, Washington, DC, September 2010.

23. Annie Lowrey, "Help Wanted," ForeignPolicy.com, January 18, 2010.

24. Hillary Rodham Clinton, Testimony Before the Senate Appropriations Subcommittee on State, Foreign Operations, and Related Programs on "The President's Proposed Budget Request for FY2011 for the Department of State and Foreign Operations," February 24, 2010, http://www.senate.gov.

25. See "Treaties" on Thomas website, Library of Congress, http://www.thomas.gov/home/treaties/treaties.html.

26. Department of State, Office of Treaty Affairs, "Treaties and Other International Agreements Concluded During the Year," May 2010.

27. Lawmakers often shy away from another useful source of information—foreign trips—because the American press has labeled them as "junkets." But most overseas visits are an excellent means to get a first-hand understanding of the conduct and impact of U.S. policy around the globe.

28. Norman J. Ornstein, Thomas E. Mann, and Michael J. Malbin, *Vital Statistics on Congress 2008* (Washington, DC: The Brookings Institution, 2008), p. 110.

29. See R. Eric Petersen, Parker H. Reynolds, and Amber Hope Wilhelm, "House of Representatives and Senate Staff Levels in Member, Committee, Leadership, and Other Offices, 1977–2010," Congressional Research Service, August 10, 2010, pp. 20–22 and 26–28.

30. For Department of Defense data, see *Washington Post*, "Top Secret America: Department of Defense HQ (DOD HQ)," July 2010; for Department of State data, see "Careers Representing America: General Information: About the U.S. Department of State," U.S. Department of State, http://careers.state.gov/general/about-us.html; for USAID data, Office of Human Resources, USAID, October 19, 2010; and for intelligence community data, see Dana Priest and William M. Arkin, "Top Secret America: A Hidden World, Growing Beyond Control," *Washington Post*, July 19, 2010.

31. For data on Senate tenure, see "A Chronological List of Senators from the First Congress to the 111th Congress," U.S. Senate, www.senate.gov/artandhistory/history/resources/pdf/chronlist.pdf; for data on House tenure, see "Seniority List of the United States House of Representatives, 111th Congress, June 14, 2010," U.S. House of Representatives, clerk.house.gov/member_info/111_seniority.pdf; and for information on retirements, vacancies, etc. in the 111th Congress prior to elections, see "111th Congress: Members in Transition," *CQ Politics*, September 2010, http://www.cqpolitics.com/wmspage.cfm?parm1=40.

32. Senate Resolution 416, "Amending the Standing Rules of the Senate to provide for cloture to be invoked with less than a three-fifths majority after additional debate," 111th Congress (2010).

33. Norman Ornstein, "A Filibuster Fix," *New York Times*, August 27, 2010.

34. For an expansive set of guidelines for good consultation, see Lee H. Hamilton with Jordan Tama, *A Creative Tension: The Foreign Policy Roles of the President and Congress* (Baltimore, MD: Johns Hopkins University Press, 2002), pp. 86–91.

35. Hamilton with Tama, p. 71.

About the Author

Kay King is vice president of Washington Initiatives at the Council on Foreign Relations (CFR). King joined CFR from the Center for Strategic and International Studies (CSIS), where she was vice president for external relations, responsible for leading strategic communications and managing the center's interactions with Congress, the executive branch, the media, and the international policy community.

Before joining CSIS, she served as director of congressional and public affairs at the U.S. Institute of Peace, as president of King Strategies, and as deputy assistant secretary of state for legislative affairs. She was also the first executive director of the Association of Professional Schools of International Affairs and a senior legislative assistant for foreign and defense policy to Senator Joseph R. Biden Jr. (D-DE).

King received a BA from Vassar College and an MA from Columbia University's School of International and Public Affairs.

Advisory Committee for
Congress and National Security

Council Special Reports

Published by the Council on Foreign Relations

Toward Deeper Reductions in U.S. and Russian Nuclear Weapons
Micah Zenko; CSR No. 57, November 2010
A Center for Preventive Action Report

Internet Governance in an Age of Cyber Insecurity
Robert K. Knake; CSR 56, September 2010
An International Institutions and Global Governance Program Report

From Rome to Kampala: The U.S. Approach to the 2010 International Criminal Court Review Conference
Vijay Padmanabhan; CSR No. 55, April 2010

Strengthening the Nuclear Nonproliferation Regime
Paul Lettow; CSR No. 54, April 2010
An International Institutions and Global Governance Program Report

The Russian Economic Crisis
Jeffrey Mankoff; CSR No. 53, April 2010

Somalia: A New Approach
Bronwyn E. Bruton; CSR No. 52, March 2010
A Center for Preventive Action Report

The Future of NATO
James M. Goldgeier; CSR No. 51, February 2010
An International Institutions and Global Governance Program Report

The United States in the New Asia
Evan A. Feigenbaum and Robert A. Manning; CSR No. 50, November 2009
An International Institutions and Global Governance Program Report

Intervention to Stop Genocide and Mass Atrocities: International Norms and U.S. Policy
Matthew C. Waxman; CSR No. 49, October 2009
An International Institutions and Global Governance Program Report

Enhancing U.S. Preventive Action
Paul B. Stares and Micah Zenko; CSR No. 48, October 2009
A Center for Preventive Action Report

The Canadian Oil Sands: Energy Security vs. Climate Change
Michael A. Levi; CSR No. 47, May 2009
A Maurice R. Greenberg Center for Geoeconomic Studies Report

The National Interest and the Law of the Sea
Scott G. Borgerson; CSR No. 46, May 2009

Lessons of the Financial Crisis
Benn Steil; CSR No. 45, March 2009
A Maurice R. Greenberg Center for Geoeconomic Studies Report

Global Imbalances and the Financial Crisis
Steven Dunaway; CSR No. 44, March 2009
A Maurice R. Greenberg Center for Geoeconomic Studies Report

Eurasian Energy Security
Jeffrey Mankoff; CSR No. 43, February 2009

Preparing for Sudden Change in North Korea
Paul B. Stares and Joel S. Wit; CSR No. 42, January 2009
A Center for Preventive Action Report

Averting Crisis in Ukraine
Steven Pifer; CSR No. 41, January 2009
A Center for Preventive Action Report

Congo: Securing Peace, Sustaining Progress
Anthony W. Gambino; CSR No. 40, October 2008
A Center for Preventive Action Report

Deterring State Sponsorship of Nuclear Terrorism
Michael A. Levi; CSR No. 39, September 2008

China, Space Weapons, and U.S. Security
Bruce W. MacDonald; CSR No. 38, September 2008

Sovereign Wealth and Sovereign Power: The Strategic Consequences of American Indebtedness
Brad W. Setser; CSR No. 37, September 2008
A Maurice R. Greenberg Center for Geoeconomic Studies Report

Securing Pakistan's Tribal Belt
Daniel Markey; CSR No. 36, July 2008 (Web-only release) and August 2008
A Center for Preventive Action Report

Avoiding Transfers to Torture
Ashley S. Deeks; CSR No. 35, June 2008

Global FDI Policy: Correcting a Protectionist Drift
David M. Marchick and Matthew J. Slaughter; CSR No. 34, June 2008
A Maurice R. Greenberg Center for Geoeconomic Studies Report

Dealing with Damascus: Seeking a Greater Return on U.S.-Syria Relations
Mona Yacoubian and Scott Lasensky; CSR No. 33, June 2008
A Center for Preventive Action Report

Climate Change and National Security: An Agenda for Action
Joshua W. Busby; CSR No. 32, November 2007
A Maurice R. Greenberg Center for Geoeconomic Studies Report

Planning for Post-Mugabe Zimbabwe
Michelle D. Gavin; CSR No. 31, October 2007
A Center for Preventive Action Report

The Case for Wage Insurance
Robert J. LaLonde; CSR No. 30, September 2007
A Maurice R. Greenberg Center for Geoeconomic Studies Report

Reform of the International Monetary Fund
Peter B. Kenen; CSR No. 29, May 2007
A Maurice R. Greenberg Center for Geoeconomic Studies Report

Nuclear Energy: Balancing Benefits and Risks
Charles D. Ferguson; CSR No. 28, April 2007

Nigeria: Elections and Continuing Challenges
Robert I. Rotberg; CSR No. 27, April 2007
A Center for Preventive Action Report

The Economic Logic of Illegal Immigration
Gordon H. Hanson; CSR No. 26, April 2007
A Maurice R. Greenberg Center for Geoeconomic Studies Report

The United States and the WTO Dispute Settlement System
Robert Z. Lawrence; CSR No. 25, March 2007
A Maurice R. Greenberg Center for Geoeconomic Studies Report

Bolivia on the Brink
Eduardo A. Gamarra; CSR No. 24, February 2007
A Center for Preventive Action Report

After the Surge: The Case for U.S. Military Disengagement from Iraq
Steven N. Simon; CSR No. 23, February 2007

Darfur and Beyond: What Is Needed to Prevent Mass Atrocities
Lee Feinstein; CSR No. 22, January 2007

Avoiding Conflict in the Horn of Africa: U.S. Policy Toward Ethiopia and Eritrea
Terrence Lyons; CSR No. 21, December 2006
A Center for Preventive Action Report

Living with Hugo: U.S. Policy Toward Hugo Chávez's Venezuela
Richard Lapper; CSR No. 20, November 2006
A Center for Preventive Action Report

Reforming U.S. Patent Policy: Getting the Incentives Right
Keith E. Maskus; CSR No. 19, November 2006
A Maurice R. Greenberg Center for Geoeconomic Studies Report

Foreign Investment and National Security: Getting the Balance Right
Alan P. Larson and David M. Marchick; CSR No. 18, July 2006
A Maurice R. Greenberg Center for Geoeconomic Studies Report

Challenges for a Postelection Mexico: Issues for U.S. Policy
Pamela K. Starr; CSR No. 17, June 2006 (Web-only release) and November 2006

U.S.-India Nuclear Cooperation: A Strategy for Moving Forward
Michael A. Levi and Charles D. Ferguson; CSR No. 16, June 2006

Generating Momentum for a New Era in U.S.-Turkey Relations
Steven A. Cook and Elizabeth Sherwood-Randall; CSR No. 15, June 2006

Peace in Papua: Widening a Window of Opportunity
Blair A. King; CSR No. 14, March 2006
A Center for Preventive Action Report

Neglected Defense: Mobilizing the Private Sector to Support Homeland Security
Stephen E. Flynn and Daniel B. Prieto; CSR No. 13, March 2006

Afghanistan's Uncertain Transition From Turmoil to Normalcy
Barnett R. Rubin; CSR No. 12, March 2006
A Center for Preventive Action Report

Preventing Catastrophic Nuclear Terrorism
Charles D. Ferguson; CSR No. 11, March 2006

Getting Serious About the Twin Deficits
Menzie D. Chinn; CSR No. 10, September 2005
A Maurice R. Greenberg Center for Geoeconomic Studies Report

Both Sides of the Aisle: A Call for Bipartisan Foreign Policy
Nancy E. Roman; CSR No. 9, September 2005

Forgotten Intervention? What the United States Needs to Do in the Western Balkans
Amelia Branczik and William L. Nash; CSR No. 8, June 2005
A Center for Preventive Action Report

A New Beginning: Strategies for a More Fruitful Dialogue with the Muslim World
Craig Charney and Nicole Yakatan; CSR No. 7, May 2005

Power-Sharing in Iraq
David L. Phillips; CSR No. 6, April 2005
A Center for Preventive Action Report

Giving Meaning to "Never Again": Seeking an Effective Response to the Crisis in Darfur and Beyond
Cheryl O. Igiri and Princeton N. Lyman; CSR No. 5, September 2004

Freedom, Prosperity, and Security: The G8 Partnership with Africa: Sea Island 2004 and Beyond
J. Brian Atwood, Robert S. Browne, and Princeton N. Lyman; CSR No. 4, May 2004

Addressing the HIV/AIDS Pandemic: A U.S. Global AIDS Strategy for the Long Term
Daniel M. Fox and Princeton N. Lyman; CSR No. 3, May 2004
Cosponsored with the Milbank Memorial Fund

Challenges for a Post-Election Philippines
Catharin E. Dalpino; CSR No. 2, May 2004
A Center for Preventive Action Report

Stability, Security, and Sovereignty in the Republic of Georgia
David L. Phillips; CSR No. 1, January 2004
A Center for Preventive Action Report

To purchase a printed copy, call the Brookings Institution Press: 800.537.5487.
Note: Council Special Reports are available for download from CFR's website, www.cfr.org.
For more information, email publications@cfr.org.